A Great Idea
ENGINEERING

The Hoover Dam

By Heather Miller

Norwood House Press

Cover: The Pat Tillman Bridge Bypass and Hoover Dam.

Norwood House Press
P.O. Box 316598
Chicago, Illinois 60631

For information regarding Norwood House Press, please visit our Web site at:
www.norwoodhousepress.com or call 866-565-2900.

PHOTO CREDITS: Cover: © Julie Quarry / Alamy; © AP Images, 17, 35; © Bettman/Corbis, 21; © Bettman/Corbis/AP Images, 23; Bow Editorial Services, 8, 19, 30, 38; © Byron Jorjorian/Alamy, 40; © Corbis, 29; © DIZ Muenchen Gmbh, Sueddeutsche Zeitung Photo/Alamy, 12, 25, 33; © Everett Collection, Inc./Alamy, 18; © General Photographic Agency/Getty Images, 5; © Jim Parkin/ Alamy, 31; © Julie Mowbray/Alamy, 6; © Popperfoto/Getty Image, 9, 15, 20; © PTLee/Alamy, 42; © Robert Harding World Imagery/Alamy, 39

LIBRARY OF CONGRESS CATALOGING-IN-PUBLICATION DATA

Miller, Heather.
The Hoover Dam / by Heather Miller
pages cm. -- (A great idea)
Summary: "Describes the struggles and accomplishments in building the Hoover Dam. Includes glossary, websites, and bibliography for further reading"--Provided by publisher.
Includes index.
ISBN 978-1-59953-595-1 (library edition : alkaline paper)
ISBN 978-1-60357-588-1 (ebook)
1. Hoover Dam (Ariz. and Nev.)--Juvenile literature. 2. Dams--Colorado River (Colo.-Mexico)--Design and construction--Juvenile literature. I. Title.
TC557.5.H6M45 2013
627'.80979159--dc23

2013011169

Manufactured in the United States of America in North Mankato, Minnesota.
233N—072013

Contents

Note: Words that are **bolded** in the text are defined in the glossary.

Chapter 1

Taming a River

The Colorado River once flowed freely across the western United States. Each spring it thundered through the deserts of the Southwest. The river often flooded towns and destroyed crops. The river seemed wild. In the early 1900s people started to wonder whether it could be tamed. Engineers began to research. They wanted to build a wall that could trap the river. So they made a plan to build a dam. The dam would control flooding. It would also provide water for crops and generate electrical power for millions of people living in the Southwest.

Danger and Destruction

The dam site was located in a canyon about 30 miles (48km) south of Las Vegas, Nevada. The name of the canyon is Black Canyon. It is a rugged place that gets as hot as 130°F (54°C). In the

Black Canyon, 30 miles (48km) south of Las Vegas, Nevada, was chosen for the site of Hoover Dam.

winter Black Canyon is blasted by icy winds and pelted by freezing rain. The area is so extreme it is hard for humans to tolerate unless they have shelter. The jagged rocks and steep cliffs are not places where people would choose to live and work. Workers needed to be strong and able to withstand extreme temperatures. Building a dam in the Black Canyon would be dangerous.

The Colorado River's raging rapids were studied by engineers to learn how to control them.

The Colorado River was not an easy river to control. It flowed with raging rapids. Engineers studied the river to learn how to control it. Each spring the snow on the tops of mountains in Colorado, Wyoming, and Utah begins to melt. The melting snow flows down the mountains. As more snow melts, more water flows. Tiny trickles of water combine with mountain streams. Mountain streams combine with small rivers. Smaller rivers connect to the Colorado River. All the water combines together and sends a rush of water down the Colorado River. The river squeezes through canyons. When the river is squeezed, the currents rush even faster. When this happens, floods can occur. During a flood, the river can rise 17 feet (5m) in just one hour. A flood that powerful can quickly destroy homes and crops. It can also endanger lives.

Did You Know?

There are 53 dams along the Colorado River. The Hoover Dam is the largest.

Before the Hoover Dam was built, Colorado River floods destroyed crops and homes. In 1905 a great flood ruined millions of acres of crops. When the floods dried up, the land was left dry. During the summer little water could be found. Farmers could not grow crops in these conditions. They needed a way to control the water so they could water their crops evenly and when they needed water most.

A Simple Design

Plans for the Hoover Dam showed a need to control trillions of gallons of rushing water. The dam needed to be strong, and it needed to last. Engineers set to work to design a dam that would be strong enough to control the Colorado River. Finally, they solved the problem and decided to design an arch dam.

Arch dams are very strong. They use the laws of **physics** to increase their strength. An arch dam is curved, like

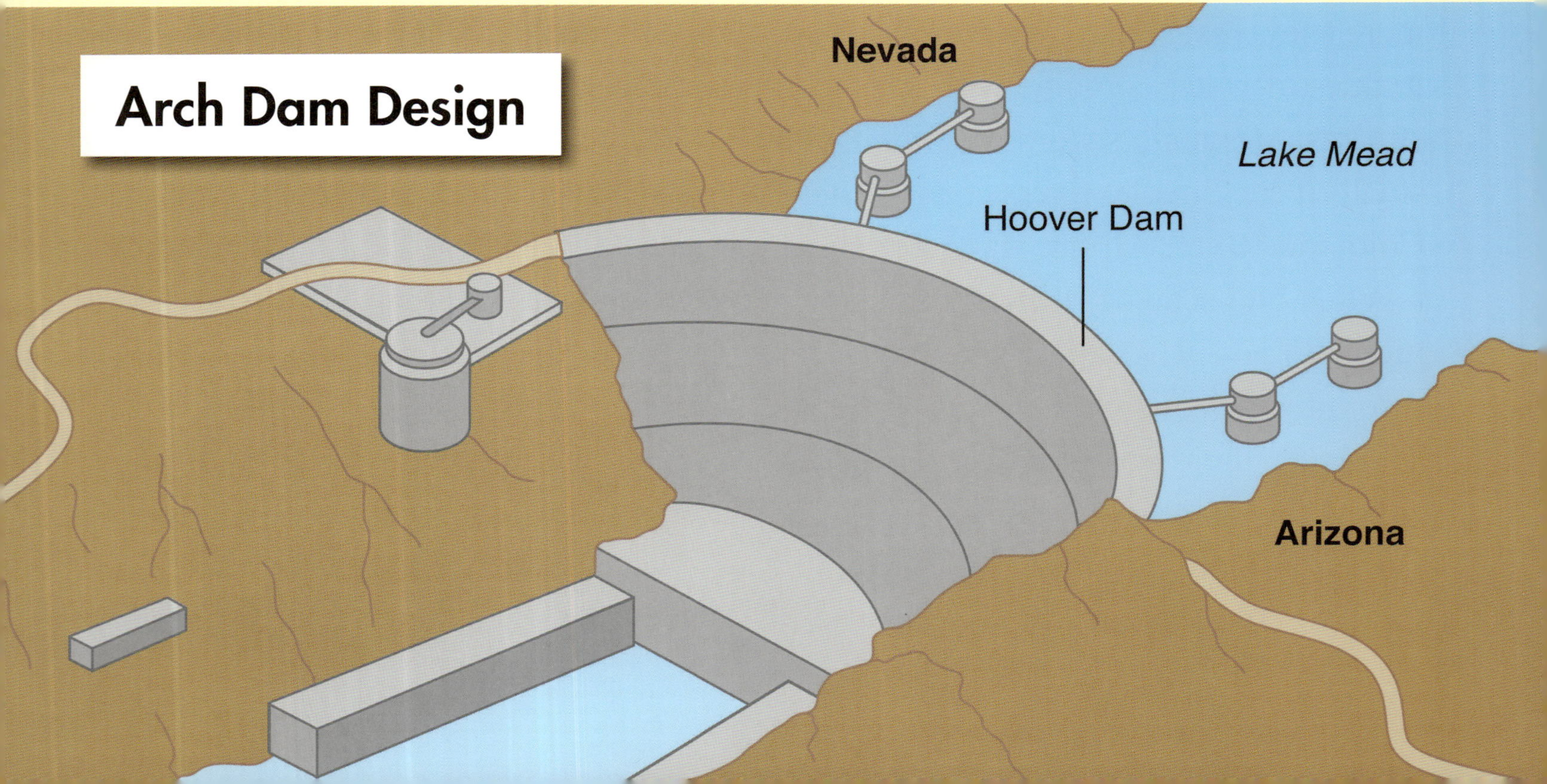

a bow that shoots an arrow. The dam is wide at the top and narrow at the bottom. It curves toward the water it holds back. The pressure from the river current pushes against the curved dam. The walls of the dam press against the canyon walls. The canyon walls hold the dam firm, sending pressure back into it. Together the laws of physics and gravity create an incredibly strong wall. The Hoover Dam's simple design is very efficient.

The walls of Black Canyon were rugged and steep. Before the dam could be built, the rocks needed to be shaped. Engineers set to work to figure out how to smooth the canyon walls in order to make room for the dam. They were careful to design a dam that could fit between the cliffs.

Before the dam could be built, the rocks of Black Canyon needed to be shaped so that the dam would fit between the cliffs.

A Chance for Work

Designing the dam was only the first step in taming the Colorado River. Thousands of workers needed to be hired. But there were no towns or homes nearby for workers to live in. Resources needed to be brought to the area. Railways needed to be built. Roads needed to be made. There was no electricity or plumbing in place.

Even though there was no place to live, workers rushed to help with the construction of the dam. Men in the United States needed jobs. At the time the Hoover Dam was built, the United States was suffering through the Great Depression. During this time many people lost their jobs. People were poor and struggled to find enough money to buy food. When the chance to work on the Hoover Dam was announced, families traveled west. They knew the work would be hard, but they were willing to do it. The construction of the Hoover Dam would provide the United States with a symbol of hope. The Great Depression made people feel like the country would never recover. The dam proved that with hard work people could accomplish great things, even in times of hardship.

Building a City

Men looking for work brought their wives and children. When they realized there were no homes to live in, families set up tents and shelters made of cardboard and other simple materials. These areas became known as tent cities. Sanitation in tent cities was poor. There was little clean water. Life in the tent cities was very hard. If the men and families were to stay safe and healthy, something needed to change quickly. A town had to be built to keep the workers and their families happy, strong, and safe.

The town was called Boulder City. Boulder City was built as a temporary city. Its purpose was to serve as a home for the workers who built the Hoover Dam. The construction companies in charge of the Hoover Dam built a school, a post office, several churches, a library, a newspaper company, and even a movie theater. They created a system to bring in clean water and electricity. The town was simple. But it was much better than the tent city. With a town in place, workers could focus on the job at hand.

Six Companies, Inc.

The Hoover Dam was built by many partnerships. Even the company that provided the workers for the project was made up of partnerships. Before construction could start on the dam, the government put out a call for companies to take on the job. The government required the company to put up $2 million to prove that it had the resources to do the job. At the time, the United States was struggling through the Great Depression. No one company could gather $2 million. So a partnership was created. Six large construction companies partnered to form a new company called Six Companies, Inc. They worked together to complete the dam. They finished the project two years ahead of schedule.

Boulder City

The desert wasteland that became Boulder City changed quickly. In just one year, 1,000 homes were built. To support the families living in those homes, other buildings were also put up. Workers built four churches, a grade school, shops, restaurants, and a 700-seat theater. During the five years that dam construction took place, Boulder City was a very safe place to live. Only one major crime occurred. Two criminals robbed the theater. The criminals were caught within two hours. The remainder of the time, families lived without fear of crime.

Thousands of houses were built in Boulder City near the dam to house workers and their families.

More Preparations

Besides workers, the Hoover Dam required materials. Massive amounts of concrete would be used. There were no concrete plants anywhere near the dam site. So a factory needed to be built. A pipe-making plant was also needed. Roads and railways were laid down to help bring in necessary materials.

Bringing in materials was a basic need for the construction. But before any materials could be used, the river had to be controlled. Workers could not build a dam in a wild river. Workers and engineers needed to find a way to divert, or change the course of, the river so that construction could begin.

Chapter 2

Building a Wall

The Hoover Dam is an example of what hard work and engineering can achieve. The huge concrete wall built across the Black Canyon holds back the Colorado River. Behind the dam sits a human-made lake, Lake Mead. Today Lake Mead is the largest human-made lake in the United States.

Did You Know?

The Colorado River is more than 1,400 miles (2,253km) long. It is the third-longest river in the United States.

Digging the Tunnels

The creation of the dam took planning and preparation. Before construction could start, a dry work area was made. The Colorado River was moved from its usual course. Engineers found a way to

In order to begin construction the course of the Colorado River had to be diverted through four huge tunnels dug into the walls of Black Canyon.

make the river flow off to the sides of the canyon and out of the way of the construction. In order to do this, four huge tunnels were dug into the walls of Black Canyon. The plan was to send the river rushing through these tunnels. When the dam was finished, the river could be returned to its normal course. The tunnels made for this task were called diversion tunnels.

Each diversion tunnel was 56 feet (17m) in **diameter** and 4,000 feet (1.2km) long. A four-story building could stand inside a tunnel that large. Digging away at rock and dirt was hard to do. When the job began, no roads had been built down into the canyon. Equipment, men, and supplies had to be brought to the worksite on boats.

Large trucks, called jumbo trucks, were built for the job. Jumbo trucks were equipped with three levels of drilling platforms. Each platform held dozens of workers. Using a jumbo truck, workers could dig the top, middle, and bottom of the diversion tunnel all at once. The men dug blasting holes, up to 30 holes at a time. The blasting holes were filled with dynamite. After all the holes were filled, the jumbo trucks rolled away from the tunnel. The blast was **detonated**, and tons of rock and dirt were blown away from the canyon walls. Workers filled giant dump trucks with the loose rock and soil. Slowly but surely, the diversion tunnels grew larger and longer.

Working Around the Clock

Three shifts of men worked around the clock to build the diversion tunnels. Once roads were finished, workers traveled to the worksite on double-decker buses. Sharpening shops worked 24 hours a day to keep drill bits sharp. It was important to keep the work moving. Workers were pressured to work, even when temperatures grew dangerously high. It often got as hot as 120°F (49°C). Fourteen men lost their lives from heat exhaustion while

Each diversion tunnel was 56 feet (17m) wide and 4,000 feet (1.2km) long.

Hard Hats

The Hoover Dam project was the first construction project that required workers to wear hard hats. The construction company in charge, Six Companies, purchased these for all of the workers. No worker was allowed to enter the canyon without a hard hat. One example of a worker who was saved from injury by wearing a hard hat involved a carpenter. The carpenter was hit on the head by a large piece of lumber. His hard hat was dented. The worker was not injured and went back to his duties soon after the accident.

Hard hat–wearing workers drill holes for blasting. The Hoover Dam project was the first construction project to require workers to wear hard hats.

building the diversion tunnels. Even so, more men were eager to take their places.

The workers who blasted away rock were followed by other workers who lined the tunnel walls with concrete. The tunnels were lined with concrete to prevent the holes from caving in. Special equipment was used to build 3-foot-thick (91cm) walls inside each tunnel. The base of the wall was built first. Moveable steel forms pushed along the tunnel walls on rail tracks. The forms held the concrete in place as it dried.

After the base was poured, the workers added the sidewalls. Finally, a concrete gun was used to shoot wet concrete at the tunnel ceiling. With the top arch of the tunnel finished, the tunnels were complete. In just fourteen months, workers had accomplished the first major task of building the Hoover Dam.

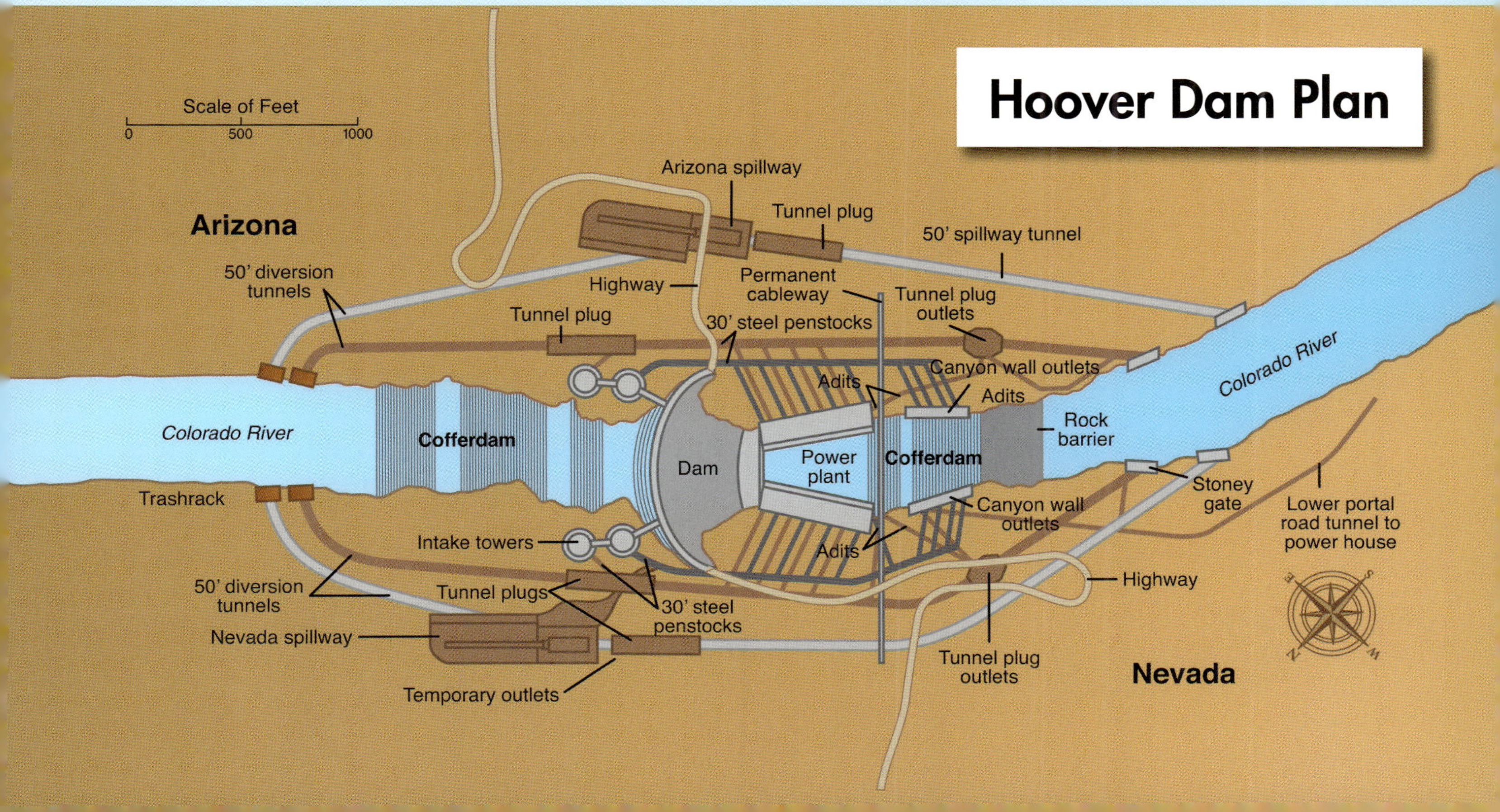

High scalers drilled holes in the surface of the rock that were later filled with dynamite. With each blast the shape of the dam began to form.

In November 1932 the Colorado River's course was changed by humans. Bulldozers pushed rock and dirt into a giant pile. The pile was called a cofferdam. The cofferdam pushed the river off course and through the diversion tunnels. Another cofferdam was built on the other side of the dam site to keep the river from washing back into the work zone. Pumps were used to remove the rest of the water. At last a dry work area had been made. Now the real construction of the dam could start.

A Solid Foundation

First, a solid foundation was built. The process involved many steps. The canyon was cleared and shaped with dynamite. Workers called "high scalers" moved along the canyon walls like acrobats. They sat on contraptions similar to playground swings. Long ropes,

Large fleets of dump trucks were needed to help remove over 2 million cubic yards (1,529,110 cubic meters) of dirt and rock.

secured at the top of the canyon, connected to wooden platforms that were like swing seats. The high scalers sat on the seats. High scalers swung side to side and crawled up and down the canyon walls. They drilled holes in the rock.

Other workers, called powder monkeys, followed the high scalers. Powder monkeys filled each drill hole with dynamite. After all the holes were filled, workers in the canyon took shelter. Then the blasts were set off. After each blast, high scalers dropped down again and removed the loosened rock that stuck to the sides of the canyon. The sides of the canyon were smoothed and carefully formed into a V shape to fit the dam's special design.

At the bottom of the canyon, workers used steam shovels to dig through dirt and rock. They needed to clear an area of **bedrock**, which would support the dam's foundation. Digging to bedrock was a huge task. Workers had to dig down more than 135 feet (41m). That's about the same height as a water tower. They removed more than 2 million cubic yards (1.5 million cubic meters) of dirt. Transporting waste from the worksite was a problem. Fleets of large dump trucks loaded and carried away dirt. The trucks dumped the dirt and rock into waiting railcars. Railcars took the dirt away and unloaded it in smaller side canyons. Workers continued day and night, clearing away a 40-foot-deep (12m) section of the riverbed.

Once an area of bedrock was exposed, great care was taken to prepare the surface. Power washers removed the final bits of loose rock and soil. Small cracks in the bedrock were sealed to stop water from seeping through. More drainage pipes were set up to keep the worksite dry. Every step was taken to build a solid foundation for the Hoover Dam.

Making the Concrete

The dam and its foundation were constructed from concrete. The production of concrete was done carefully. Proper

Concrete-mixing plants capable of mixing 100,000 cubic yards (76,455 cubic meters) of concrete per month were used to produce concrete for the dam.

amounts of sand, lime, and other minerals needed to be mixed just right. Low-quality concrete might allow the dam to collapse.

Twelve miles (19km) from the dam site, in Arizona, a streambed served as the concrete production site. Sand and gravel was dug from the dry streambed. Sand and rock were put on a train and taken to an **aggregate** plant. At the plant the sand and rock was first washed. After washing, it was sorted by size. Workers used machines to drop rock and sand into hoppers, or containers. Conveyor belts moved the rock along to machines called gobbles.

At the gobbles, the rocks and sand passed through screens. The largest rocks were captured by the screens and taken by conveyor belts to be crushed into smaller rocks. Four sizes of rock were sorted and put into piles. Sand was sorted into three sizes of grit. These were the ingredients that would be used to mix concrete. The mixtures of concrete changed according to the purpose the concrete would serve.

Concrete is a specific recipe of limestone, clay, shale, and gypsum. When mixing concrete for the Hoover Dam, conveyor belts loaded the required amounts of sand and gravel onto rail cars. Much like making a cake, the ingredients needed to be carefully measured. Because the concrete needed to be made perfectly, machines were used to measure and mix it. Mechanically **calibrated** machines took away the risk of human error. As long as the machines worked properly, the concrete could be mixed with precision.

Concrete was needed at the top of the canyon and at the bottom. For this reason, there were two mixing plants. Various types of containers were used to transport the concrete. Some concrete needed to be mixed during transport. Trains transported most concrete in powder form.

Pouring the Concrete

On June 6, 1933, the first load of concrete was poured at the dam. The dam is not made of one solid chunk of concrete. Instead, it was made of individually poured blocks. Each block of the dam was shaped by a simple mold called a form. The forms were made with wood placed in the shape of squares and rectangles. Much like giant sandboxes, the forms provided edges so that the concrete could dry within a shape without flowing over the edges.

Each form created a block between 25 feet (7.6m) and 60 feet (18m) across. After the concrete was partly dry, the wooden forms were removed. Grout, a type of thick cement, was used to fill in the spaces between the concrete blocks. After completing one set of blocks, the forms were moved and rebuilt in new places. Then the process began again.

Concrete construction continued 24 hours a day. Cableways were constructed

Hoover Dam was constructed of individually poured concrete blocks made using simple wooden molds.

to move concrete to different parts of the dam. The cableways carried giant buckets loaded with concrete. The buckets whizzed across the canyon.

The process of moving concrete across the cableways was very efficient. It was also dramatic to watch. First, cranes picked up the containers from trains and trucks. Next, cable operators moved each bucket along the cable and into the canyon. Operators carefully lowered each bucket over a concrete form. Workers below received and guided each bucket into place. Safety latches were released, and 16 tons (14.5t) of concrete spilled into the form. The concrete was thick and heavy. Workers wearing high rubber boots stomped the oozing mixture into place. They used long, vibrating rods to shake air bubbles to the surface. Each day 1,100 buckets of concrete were emptied into forms.

It was necessary to build the dam with many concrete blocks rather than one huge block. As concrete dries, or cures, a chemical reaction creates heat. If the concrete for the dam had been poured all at once, it would have taken 125 years to harden and cool. Further, the uneven cooling would have caused the concrete to crack. A cracked dam could leak and worse, crumble. A solid block dam would have been a disaster.

Block by Block

To keep construction on schedule, a concrete cooling system was created. Water pipes were buried inside each concrete block. Cold water rushed through the pipes

Crossing the Border

In all, 96 men died while building the Hoover Dam. These men were issued death certificates. But these certificates could lead to some confusion. The Hoover Dam straddles the border of two states, Nevada and Arizona. If a worker died on the job, his death certificate was issued by the state he was in at the time he was injured. The families of workers with certificates from Arizona got better benefits. So workers often moved bodies to Arizona's side. Injured workers did the same. They often crawled or moved to the Arizona side so they could get better care.

to help the concrete cool. Thermometers measured the temperature of the cooling concrete. When the temperature was right, the next blocks were poured. If the concrete was not cool enough, heat could be trapped inside. This would cause the blocks to crack. Careful observation and patience was needed to create a strong and solid dam. Even when some workers wanted to move faster, it was important to do the job carefully and properly. The dam had to be strong and built to last.

Bit by bit, block by block, the Hoover Dam grew higher and higher. When it was finished, 582 miles (937km) of cooling pipe had been used. It took 3.25 million cubic yards (2.5 million cubic meters) of concrete to construct. The dam weighs 6.6 million tons (6 million t) and stands 726 feet (221m) tall. It is as thick as the length of two football fields. It holds back trillions of gallons of water. The wall of concrete truly is an engineering masterpiece.

Chapter 3

More than a Wall

Building a giant cement wall was just one part of the Hoover Dam project. The dam is also used to make electricity. Building the machinery to create a power plant required special materials and parts. A steel-making plant was built to make custom pipes. The plant also made other large structures. These included generators, which are used to make power. Because some of these parts were so large, it was too costly to transport them from existing factories to the dam site. Some pipes needed for the dam ranged from 8 feet (2.4m) to 30 feet (9m) in diameter. Building a factory near the dam to create these pipes was the least expensive solution.

Creating the Pipes

To create a large-diameter pipe, a machine first refined the edges of the metal. A tool called a router shaved off thin layers of metal, making the edges crisp and clean. After preparing the metal sheet in the router, a second machine heated and pressed the metal. Next, the plates were heated and rolled. This produced a curved piece of metal that took on an arch shape. Three arched plates joined together to create a full circle or ring. The rings were welded together to create pipe sections.

These large pipe sections were used for many purposes. Penstocks were the largest pipe sections. They allow water

One of the four penstocks under construction. The towers draw water to the turbines.

to flow into the generator's turbines. The turbines turn to create electricity. Each penstock weighs 160 tons (145t).

Moving these huge metal pipes into place was not an easy task. Special cranes were built for the job. The cranes moved each section of the penstock through the plant during construction. When finished, the cranes loaded each penstock onto a train or caterpillar tractor. A system of cables was used to move the penstocks into place. It was similar to the system used to move the concrete buckets. The penstocks would serve as gateways to allow water to rush in to turn the power generators' turbines.

Making Electricity

Two power plants were constructed at the Hoover Dam. One U-shaped plant

Hydro Turbine Generator

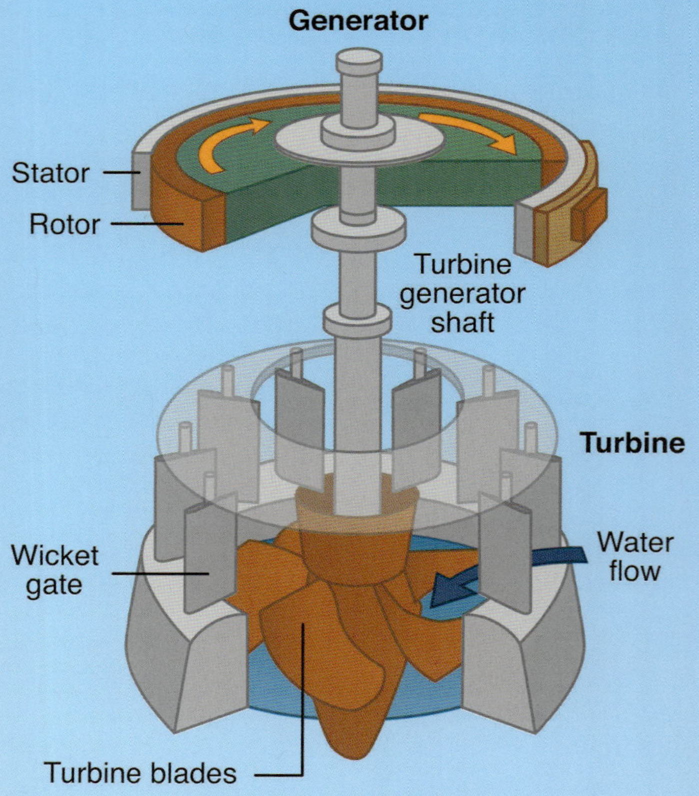

Flowing water causes the turbine blades to rotate the rotor which generates electricity.

Two power plants were constructed on either side of the dam, and seventeen generators produce electricity for over 1.7 million people.

was placed at each side of the dam. Four intake towers, two at each side of the dam, collect water from upstream. The water flows at a rapid rate, down the intake tower. At the bottom of the tower, water flows through the penstocks and into the turbines. The current of the flowing water makes the turbine blades spin at high speed.

The turbine blades cause a tall shaft, or metal rod, to rotate. The shaft is attached to a generator. When the shaft

Deadly Gas

Men who worked to dig the tunnels around the Hoover Dam were at great risk. Gasoline engines powered the trucks that carried away dirt. These engines give off carbon monoxide gas. This is a deadly gas. The tunnels often filled with the gas. This made the men get sick. Some even died. There is no official death toll for workers who lost their lives from carbon monoxide poisoning.

turns, the generator operates. Inside the generator a large wheel is lined with magnets. The wheel is called a rotor. The spinning magnets rotate along a rim of copper wires. Together the copper wires and spinning magnets make electricity. This power moves through the copper wires. The copper wires connect to power lines that carry the power to cities, home, factories, and other places that need energy.

There are seventeen generators at the Hoover Dam. Each generator produces enough power for 100,000 people. Beyond the generators, the water from upstream continues to flow through pipes called outlets. At the bottom of the dam, the water flows back into the Colorado River.

Spillways Stop Floods

To keep the Colorado River from flooding over the top of the dam, workers built spillways. Engineers designed two spill-

The turbine room was completed in 1937.

ways to prevent floods. The spillways are concrete tunnels that open 27 feet (8m) below the top of the dam. If the water on the upstream side reaches that level, the water just flows through the spillways. Then it flows into the downstream side of the river.

The spillways have only been used two times. The first time was in 1941 during a test. The second time was in 1983 during a very wet season. The spillways prevented an actual flood that year.

Did You Know?

The Hoover Dam is 660 feet (201m) thick at the base. That is about the length of the Seattle Space Needle, if it were lying on the ground.

A Symbol of Accomplishment

At last, the spillways were in place and most of the major structures were built. It was time to officially open the Hoover Dam. On September 30, 1935, the dam was dedicated. More than 12,000 people gathered. Those who had worked for years to build the dam stood by with excitement. The symbol of accomplishment was important to the entire nation. The Great Depression was a hard time for the United States. The completion of the dam showed that the United States would once again recover and **prosper**. President Franklin D. Roosevelt came from Washington, DC. He delivered a speech that inspired the nation.

There was a long day of celebration. Afterward, the president returned to Washington. The people of Boulder City went back to their homes. Men doing finishing jobs kept busy with day-to-day tasks. Behind the dam, a body of water slowly rose. The Colorado River had been tamed,

In the dedication ceremonies of September 30, 1935, President Franklin Roosevelt told the nation that the country would recover from the Great Depression and prosper.

African American Workers

The promise of work at the Hoover Dam brought hope to many American families. Not so for African American workers. Over the course of the project, only 24 workers were black. And those workers were given the hardest job. They had to work in the gravel pits, where temperatures soared well over 100°F (38°C). Black workers had to drink out of **segregated** water buckets. They were not allowed to live in Boulder City. Their homes were in the slums of Las Vegas. The black workers had to ride along a 30-mile (48km) bumpy road each day to get to work and back home again.

and behind the dam a new lake was born. Lake Mead is the **reservoir** created by the construction of the Hoover Dam. It was soon declared a National Recreation Area. It took six years for the reservoir to fill. Today millions of visitors enjoy it each year. It is a favorite place for boating, fishing, hiking, photography, and adventure.

Chapter 4

The Hoover Dam Changes a Nation

Today the water that rushes through the Hoover Dam brings power to millions of people. There are two power plants. One is on the Arizona side of the dam. The other is on the Nevada side. The power plants at the dam hold seventeen turbines. Nine turbines operate in Arizona. Eight operate in Nevada. The plants produce 4 billion kilowatt-hours of power each year. That is enough to supply the needs of 1.7 million people.

The power created by the Hoover Dam is sold. The money collected from selling power is used to pay for the construction

Did You Know?

The dam is helpful in removing silt and reduces the amount of sediment that is sent downriver.

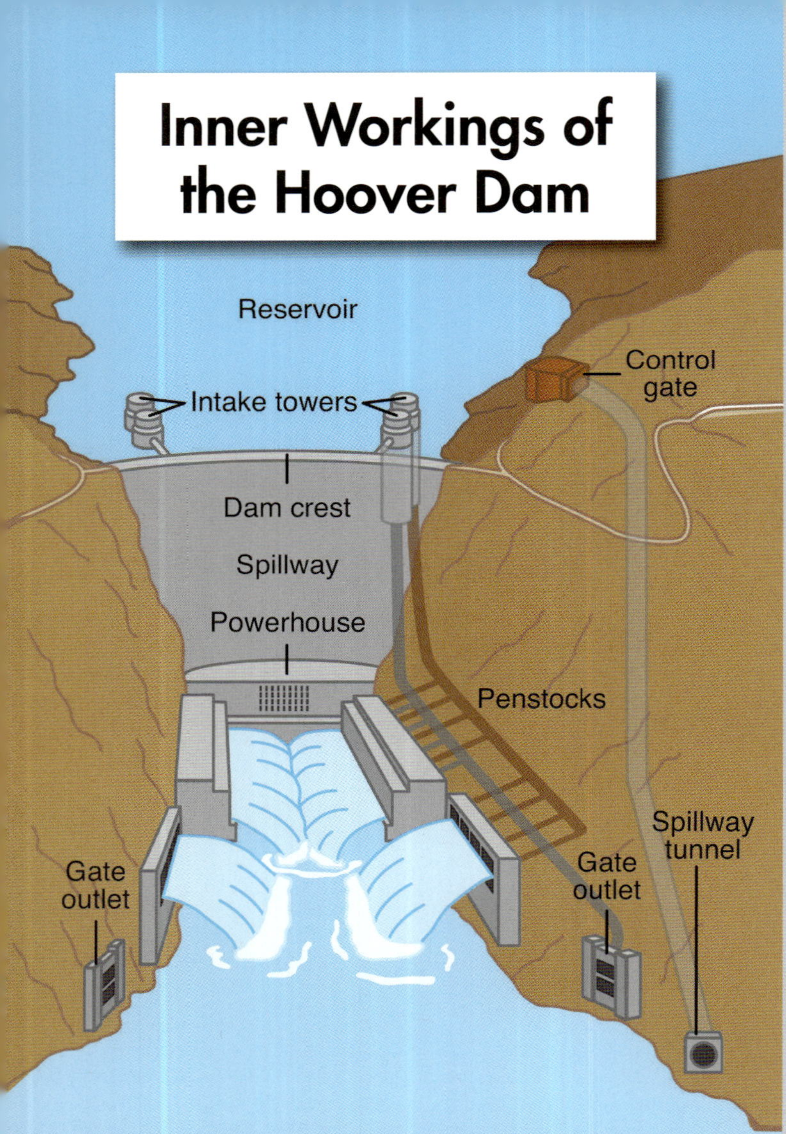

The two power plants in the Hoover Dam generate 4 billion killowatt-hours of power each year.

and upkeep of the dam. The cost of the dam construction, which was completed in 1936, was finally paid in May 1987. Any new features added to the dam after May 1987 will be fully paid for 50 years after the project is finished.

Many Uses

Making power is a major function of the Hoover Dam. But the power plants are not the main purpose of the dam. The dam was built to control the Colorado River. Since the dam was built, there have not been any floods.

The dam also helps with crop **irrigation**. The waters of the Colorado River are held back by the dam. When crops need more water, the dam can release it. The water flows downstream to sup-

The dam holds back the waters of Lake Meade. Water is released for irrigation purposes through a system of smaller canals.

ply many smaller canal systems. These systems include the Imperial Irrigation District, the All-American Canal system, and the Central Arizona Project.

The canal systems carry water to crops that need moisture. Water from Lake Mead is carried to places as far away as Mexico. More than 2 million acres (809,371ha) of land in Southern California get water from these canals. About 400,000 acres (162ha) in Mexico depend on the water supply from the Hoover Dam. The canal systems allow

Wildlife

Lake Mead has attracted many forms of wildlife. Many mammals can be found in the area. These include bighorn sheep, mule deer, coyotes, bobcats, and ringtail cats. Reptiles include the desert tortoise, lizards, and snakes. The area around Lake Mead is also home to many types of birds. These include the endangered peregrine falcon.

The formation of Lake Meade has led to a resurgence of wildlife in the area. Bighorn sheep, deer, coyotes, bobcats, and ringtail cats are just some of the animals that thrive in the area.

farmers to plant crops in places that are normally too dry to farm. The dam has turned desert land into farmland. This farmland can be used to grow large amounts food.

The Hoover Dam also provides water to people. More than 20 million people depend on the dam for water. They use this water for cooking, cleaning, and drinking. People who live in Arizona, Nevada, and Southern California use water from the dam. The dam also provides power for millions of people. It is an important structure.

Tourist Attraction

The history of the dam is rich. It is filled with stories of hardworking men and engineering feats. Each year the Hoover Dam attracts more than 1 million visitors. Tourists from all over the world visit the dam. They want to learn more about its history and to see the structure up close.

Many visitors are surprised by the dam's beauty. The designers gave a lot of attention to detail. A well-known painter named Alan True created the floor designs in the powerhouse. True used colors such as deep brown, tan, and beige. These colors capture the Native American heritage of the area. One floor design shows a Native American celestial map. The map illustrates the date September 30, 1935, at 8:56 p.m. That is the exact time when Roosevelt dedicated the dam.

The sculptor Oskar J.W. Hansen designed the elevator panels for the dam. Made from concrete, the panels illustrate five functions of the dam. Flood control, navigation, irrigation, water storage, and making power are all shown in two huge wall sculptures. Hansen also created a

Did You Know?

Lights purchased from an old baseball stadium were used to light the construction site at night.

Sculptor Oskar J.W. Hansen created the plaques honoring the 96 men who died during construction and the two statues called the *Winged Figures of the Republic.*

large plaque. It honors the 96 men who died building the dam.

Two giant sculptures also celebrate the dam's completion. Hansen created *Winged Figures of the Republic*. The proud figures stand 32 feet (9.75m) tall. They have large pointed wings that reach toward the sky. The figures are made of bronze. Together they weigh more than 40 tons (36t). The sculptures reflect the majestic power of the dam.

An Engineering Marvel

In 1995 a new visitor's center opened. The cost to build the center was more than

$1 million. The new visitor's center is a three-story glass and concrete building. It was built to project out from the canyon wall, so visitors can step out over the canyon. Inside, visitors can learn about the dam. They can see full-scale models of the buckets that carried concrete. The observation decks are popular stops for many tourists. They can look out over the dam, Lake Mead, and the Colorado River. They can imagine the men working below. And they can appreciate the hard work that was carried out to create the dam.

The Hoover Dam is no longer the largest dam in the world. But it is still an engineering marvel. Brave men built the huge wall of concrete. Families traveled across the country to follow their hope of a brighter future. The jobs that the dam created helped mothers, fathers, and children have a better life. Today the dam provides millions of people in the United States with power and water. It also keeps them safe from dangerous floods. The Hoover Dam is a human-made creation that many can be proud of. As time passes, more people will visit the dam and realize the amazing accomplishment that is the Hoover Dam.

Wages

Workers at the Hoover Dam received a range of payment. The lowest-paid workers received 50 cents per hour. Today these workers would make about $8 per hour. The highest-paid workers earned $1.25 per hour. Today those workers would earn about $20 per hour.

Glossary

aggregate [AG-gra-git]: A mixture of gravel, rock, and sand of varying sizes.

bedrock [BED-rock]: Unbroken solid rock usually covered by layers of rocks, soil, and sand.

calibrated [CAL-la-bray-ted]: Precisely set to determine and check range of measurements in order to confirm accuracy.

detonated [DET-ta-nay-ted]: Set off; exploded.

diameter [die-AM-eh-ter]: A straight line passing from one side of a circle, through its center, and to the other side.

irrigation [ear-uh-GAY-shun]: To apply water manually or mechanically to land in order to nurture plant growth.

physics [FIZ-iks]: The science of energy, force, motion and matter.

prosper [PROS-pur]: To find success, especially with money.

reservoir [REZ-er-vwar]: A place where water is stored for later use, often for drinking water, irrigation, or generation of electricity.

segregated [SEG-ri-gay-tid]: Restricted to one group, especially related to ethnic membership or race.

For More Information

Books

Jerry Borrowman, *Life and Death at Hoover Dam*. Sandy, UT: Black Canyon, 2010.

Ian Graham, *You Wouldn't Want to Work on the Hoover Dam*. New York: Franklin Watts, 2012.

Jeffrey Zuehike, *The Hoover Dam*. Minneapolis: Lerner Classroom, 2009.

Websites

Hoover Dam Factoids for Kids, Bureau of Reclamation: Lower Colorado Region www.usbr.gov/lc/hooverdam/educate/kidfacts.html

Kelly Williams, "Hoover Dam Information for Kids," eHow mom www.ehow.com/about_5380103_hoover-dam-information-kids.html

The Story of the Hoover Dam http://archive.org/details/gov.archives.arc.37058

Index

About the Author

Heather Miller works as an author, artist, and teacher in northeast Indiana. She writes books for young readers and articles for an arts magazine in her hometown. She enjoys meeting interesting people who think creatively, and she spends time reading about science and learning how the world works.